D1402486

POLICE RESCUE

EMERGENCY VEHICLES

Deborah Chancellor

A+

Smart Apple Media

Published by Smart Apple Media,
an imprint of Black Rabbit Books
P.O. Box 3263, Mankato, Minnesota 56002
www.blackrabbitbooks.com

Published by arrangement with the Watts Publishing
Group LTD, London.

Library of Congress Cataloging-in-Publication Data
Chancellor, Deborah.
 Police rescue / by Deborah Chancellor.
   p. cm. — (Emergency vehicles)
 Includes index.
 Summary: "Introduces readers to nine different
emergency vehicles, such as police cars, boats, and
helicopters, through diagramming and defining the
characteristics and emergency situations in which each is
used. Includes a reading quiz and web sites"—Provided
by publisher.
 ISBN 978-1-59920-890-9 (library binding)
 1. Police vehicles-—Juvenile literature. 2. Emergency
vehicles—Juvenile literature. I. Title.
 HV7936.V4C43 2014
 629.04'6--dc23
                              2012040045

Printed in the United States and Corporate Graphics,
North Mankato, Minnesota.

PO1585
2-2013

9 8 7 6 5 4 3 2 1

Series editor: Adrian Cole/Amy Stephenson
Editor: Sarah Ridley
Art direction: Peter Scoulding
Designer: Steve Prosser
Picture researcher: Diana Morris

Picture credits:
Paul Drabot/Shutterstock: 16-17.
edg/Shutterstock: 18.
Firebrandphotography/Dreamstime: 6-7.
David Frazier/Alamy: 5t.
Kyoungil Jeon/istockphoto: 17t.
Justin Kase/Alamy: 12-13.
KENCKOphotography/Shutterstock: front cover.
Knumina/Shutterstock: 14.
Nikolai Kovzhov/Dreamstime: 21t.
Buddy Mays/Alamy: 20-21.
Jim O'Donnell/Alamy: 13t.
Keith Pritchard/Alamy: 19.
Bernhard Richter/Dreamstime: 4-5.
rossco/Shutterstock: 9.
Brad Sauter/Dreamstime: 7b.
SHOUT/Alamy: 15.
Russell Sneddon/Alamy: 10.
Giovanni Tondelli/Shutterstock: 8.
UK Emergency Vehicles. ukemergency.co.uk: 11.

Every attempt has been made to clear copyright.
Should there be any inadvertent omission,
please apply to the publisher for rectification.

Contents

Fast Car

Police cars race to the scene of a crime.
Sirens scream and bright lights flash.

POLICE

2691

NYPD

WHEEOOO!

Police officers do not always
drive fast. When they **patrol**
an area, they drive more slowly.

4

Police officers use a small computer to check information with the police central computer.

POLICE

1558

Slow Down

A police traffic control car chases the fastest vehicles on the road. Its sirens can be heard a long way away.

WHOOEE! WHOOEE!

The police car has a built-in **camera**. This can film dangerous drivers.

The car's **radar** and **laser** equipment are both used to check speeds.

Top Speed

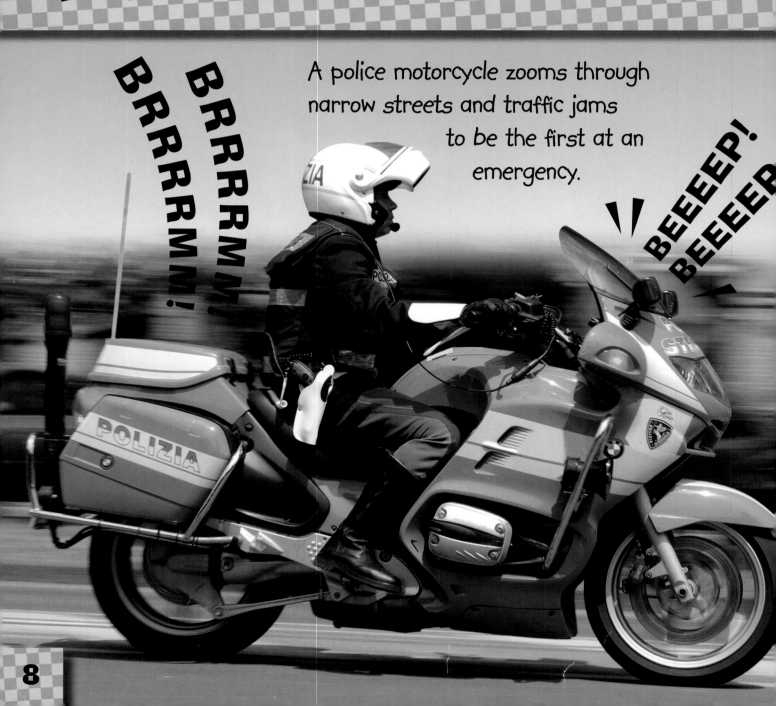

BRRRRMM!
BRRRRMM!

A police motorcycle zooms through narrow streets and traffic jams to be the first at an emergency.

BEEEEP!
BEEEEP!

Flashing lights and loud sirens make the motorcycle easy to see and hear on the road.

A **two-way radio** in the police motorcycle helmet keeps the rider in close contact with police **headquarters (HQ)**.

BRRMMMM!

9

Bumpy Trip

Police four-wheelers carry police officers over beaches and across hillsides. Wide tires make the ride less bumpy.

WOOF!

BRRRRMM!

THUMP!

BUMP!

THUMP!

A tough off-road police car is used to patrol places that can't be reached by road.

11

Van Transport

A strong police van transports equipment, prisoners, or police officers from one place to another.

The sides of a police van are strengthened to protect it. A flip-down shield stops anything from smashing the windshield.

BEEEEP! BEEEEP!

Bright markings show that this is a police van.

13

Spy in the Sky

A noisy police helicopter hovers above an **incident** on the ground. It gives backup for crowd control and high-speed car chases.

WHUPPPA!

CHUPPPA!

CHUPPA!

WHUPPPA!

Cameras are used to keep watch on a **suspect**.

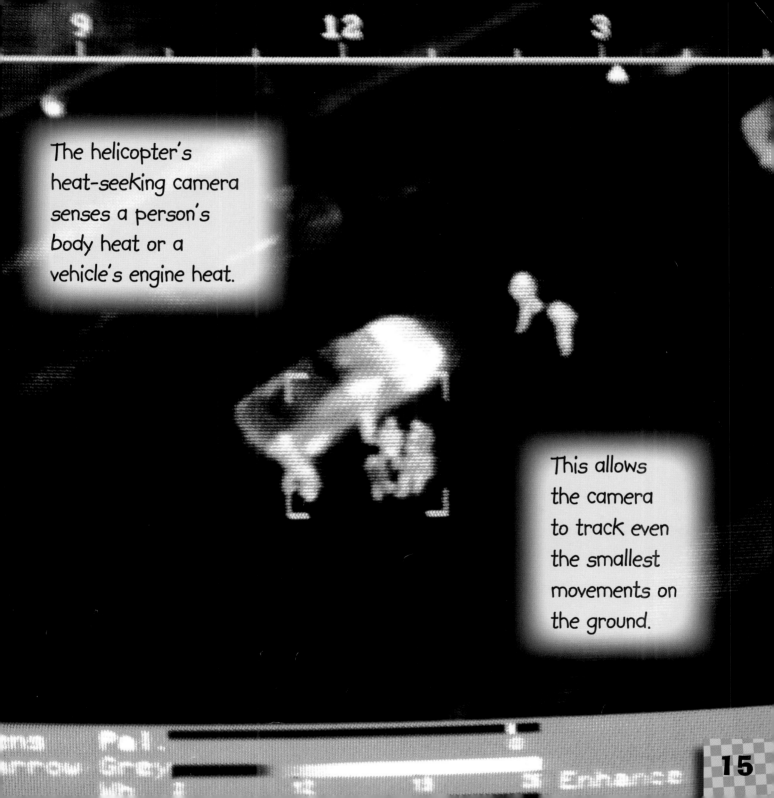

The helicopter's heat-seeking camera senses a person's body heat or a vehicle's engine heat.

This allows the camera to track even the smallest movements on the ground.

WHUPPA! CHUPPA!

Police air ambulances look for people who are lost or in danger. They can fly injured or sick people straight to the hospital.

WHUPPPA! CHUPPPA

POLICE

AMBULANCE

Searchlights and **tracking technology** help helicopters work at night.

17

Water Patrol

This police boat patrols rivers, **harbors**, and coastal waters. It has sirens and flashing lights to warn other boats to let it pass.

Police boats have powerful motors, so they can speed through choppy waters.

Radar is used to track and follow suspects.

BRUMMM!

SPLASH!

WHOOSHH!

SPLASH!

POLICE

Snow Trek

Snowmobiles are used by police in snowy areas. Police officers can drive snowmobiles deep into forests to search for missing people.

BBRRRR!

SHERIFF

ARCTIC CAT

SHERIFF

A first-aid kit is stored under the seat.

BBRRRRRRR!

BBRRRRR!

Snowmobiles have strong skis instead of wheels. Skis help them glide quickly over snow and ice.

21

Glossary

camera
police vehicles and helicopters use cameras to film suspects. Heat-seeking cameras sense movement when it is dark.

harbor
a place where boats go to shelter or unload their goods

headquarters (HQ)
the police station where police work is run from

incident
an event; either a crime or an emergency

laser
equipment that records how fast something is moving

patrol
to check an area for possible problems

radar
equipment that finds out where another car, boat, or plane is

siren
a loud hooting or wailing noise

suspect
someone who may have committed a crime

tracking technology
gadgets that help find and follow someone or something

two-way radio
a radio set you use to talk with somebody far away

Quiz

1. Do all police cars drive fast?

2. Why do the police use motorcycles?

3. What is special about a police motorcycle helmet?

4. Why do the police need off-road vehicles?

5. What are police helicopters for?

6. Why do police boats have sirens?

Answers:

1. Not all police cars drive fast. Some drive slowly to patrol an area.

2. The police use motorcycles to drive quickly through busy traffic.

3. A police motorcycle helmet has a two-way radio to keep in touch with police HQ.

4. Off-road vehicles help the police reach people in places without roads.

5. Police helicopters find and rescue people, and they watch incidents from the air.

6. Loud sirens tell other boats to move over and let the police boat speed past.

23

Index

cameras 7, 14, 15

computer 5

lights 4, 9, 18

off-road police cars 11

police
   boats 18, 19
   cars 4, 5, 6, 7
   four-wheelers 10

helicopters 14, 15, 16, 17

motorcycles 8, 9

snowmobiles 20, 21

vans 12, 13

radar 7, 19

sirens 4, 6, 9, 18

tracking technology 17

two-way radios 9

Web Sites

www.911forKids.com/

encyclopedia.kids.net.au/page/pa/Paramedic

Kidshealth.org/Kid/watch/er/911.html

WHOOEE!